J.S. BACH
Chaconne in D minor
from
Partita No. 2 BWV 1004
for
MARIMBA

Edited by

Mika Stoltzman

Special Thanks to

Yehudi Wyner
Steven Epstein
Richard Stoltzman
Douglas DeMorrow (Mika's marimba maker)
Bruce Salyers (Mika's mallet maker)
Lauren Keiser
AVIE Record (UK)
Koji Yagi

Southern
MUSIC

Note from the Editor

Preparations for this transcription began in November of 2017. As I neared the end of my work, I happened to be a page-turner f[or] Peter Serkin's Bach performance; an assignment demanding that I listen very closely to his playing. The aura that Peter created ma[de] me feel that he and the music were one as it flowed out of him. His phrasing, articulation, clarity, dynamics and delicacy of each no[te] played moved and inspired me. I wondered how I might reach those heights on marimba. With that in mind, I focused on practici[ng] the *Chaconne* until the recording session scheduled for the end of February. No gigs or concerts booked, and I even stayed awa[y] from Facebook! I practiced for hours each day, recording my playing and checking it for corrections and adjustments hundreds [of] times. I referenced all the great violin recordings available for interpretation, and even checked out arrangements for piano, guit[ar] and string quartet. I asked myself, "What if Bach were alive now and wrote this piece for marimba?" After thorough analysis of th[e] music to determine the most appropriate method of playing on my instrument, and some advice from my husband Richard and [my] composer neighbor, Yehudi Wyner, I felt that I was ready. And so, on February 28, 2018, at the Recital Hall of the Performing Ar[ts] Center in Purchase, New York, with Steven Epstein producing, my rendition of the Bach *Chaconne* on solo marimba wa[s] successfully recorded.

Performance Notes

A Bach study reads that Bach returned home one day from a long journey to find that his wife, Maria, had died accidentally, and h[e] wrote this musical monument trying to weave in his sorrow, despair and loneliness. I sympathized with his emotion from the ver[y] first note I played. Not a single note in his music being redundant, I tried to sing while playing, bearing in mind that this is a danc[e] in triple meter. In my opinion, his sorrow is best expressed in the broad arpeggio passage in the latter part of the first D minor sectio[n] of the triptych. Playing this always brings tears to my eyes. Most performers play this passage fast and quite technically, but I pla[y] it in the tempo which enables me to make emotional sonority, better reflecting his feelings and making the bass voice clearly audibl[e.] At the end of this section, the opening theme reappears. It seems as if the composer's grief is easing little by little, and at th[e] beginning of the next D major section, he starts remembering sweet days with Maria. To me, the highlight of *Chaconne* is the secon[d] theme of this section. The melody again makes me cry, so I add tremolo only to this melody line. At the last part of this D majo[r] section, I play the melody with dead stroke technique in the right hand to brighten the sound. It is here that I believe Bach i[s] encouraging himself to live on Maria's behalf. The third section in D minor is, I can imagine, a reminiscence. I apply arpeggios t[o] the first theme chords, but not to the last theme. Unlike its gloomy beginning, I think *Chaconne* ends as a kind of vigorous hymn fo[r] life.

I was so fortunate to have Yehudi Wyner give me three coaching sessions on the *Chaconne*. His wisdom and experience (He was th[e] keyboard artist for the Bach Aria Group as well as a Pulitzer Prize winning composer) was tremendously important. One of hi[s] profound, yet simple observations was to phrase with three beats per measure starting on the second beat. This revelation led me t[o] rethink my phrasing of the entire work.

Afterword

This recording is the greatest accomplishment of my life. I was pleased to hear from a listener that I am the Segovia of Marimba. [I] will be eternally grateful if my arrangement will live forever in the history of music, like that of Segovia. I still continue to practic[e] the *Chaconne* every day. Bach is so deep that new discoveries are revealed each time I play, and I consider myself fortunate to hav[e] come across music that has so profoundly changed my life.

Mika Stoltzman, Editor

Notations

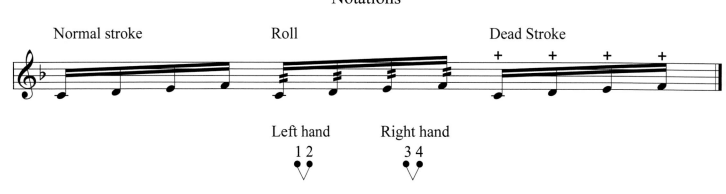

Normal stroke   Roll   Dead Stroke

Left hand   Right hand
1 2   3 4

Chaconne
for Marimba

U826

J. S. Bach

arranged by Mika Stoltzman

4

Marimba

Marimba

Marimba

7

8

Marimba

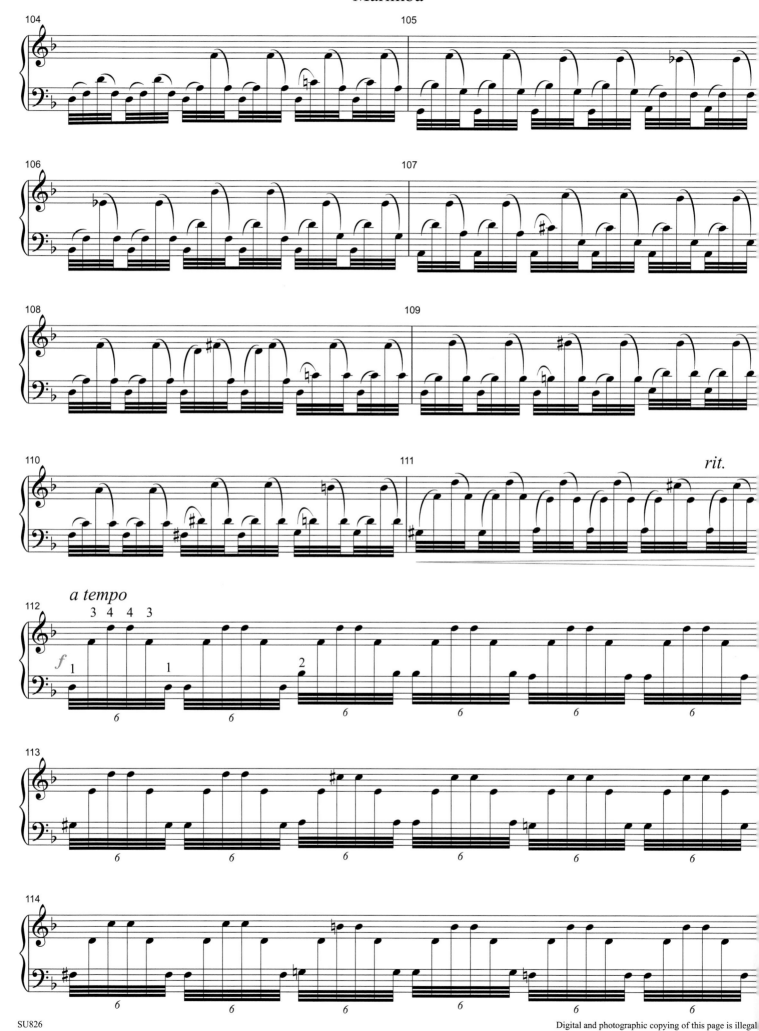

Marimba

Marimba

Marimba

Marimba

Marimba

Marimba

Mika Stoltzman recording *Chaconne* at the Purchase Performing Arts Center on February 28, 2018

Bach's *Chaconne* manuscript (beginning)

MARIMBA SOLO BESTSELLERS

SU313 Amazing Grace John Newton/ Linda Maxey

ST893 Carmen Suite Georges Bizet/ Linda Maxey

SS894 Concertino George Frock

ST747 Devil, Daniel and Duane, The Todd Ukena

ST483 Etude in d Minor Alice Gomez

SU293 Flight of the Bumblebee Rimsky-Korsakov/ Linda Maxey

ST505 Gitano Alice Gomez

SU13 Jungle Walk David E Jarvis

ST581 Lauren's Lullaby Todd Ukena

ST852 Leyenda Isaac Albeniz/ Linda Maxey

ST749 Malletrix (Mallet Tricks) Jared Spears

SU41 Marimba Flamenca Alice Gomez

SU034 Mbira Song Alice Gomez/ Marilyn Rife

ST455 Mexican Variations George Frock

ST160 Prayer Richard Gipson

ST695 Rain Dance Alice Gomez/ Marilyn Rife

SU40 Scenes from Mexico Alice Gomez

ST454 Solfeggio in c Minor C.P.E. Bach/ Sharda Brody

B339 Southern Special Marimba Solos William Schinstine

ST402 Suite Mexicana Keith Larson

ST673 Tempest Todd Ukena

SU428 Three Concert Pieces Alice Gomez

ST490 True Lover's Farewell Steven Gwin

ST281 Two Pieces Murray Houllif

ST365 Whirlwind, The George H Green/ William Schinstine

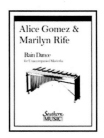

EXCLUSIVELY DISTRIBUTED BY
Hal•LEONARD®

KEISERSOUTHERNMUSIC.COM